From Egg to Adult
The Life Cycle of Reptiles

Mike Unwin

Heinemann Library
Chicago, Illinois

Customer Service 888-454-2279
Visit our website at www.heinemannlibrary.com

Editing, Design, Photo Research, and Production by Heinemann Library
Illustrations by David Woodroffe
Originated by Dot Gradations Ltd
Printed in China by Wing King Tong

07 06 05 04 03
10 9 8 7 6 5 4 3 2 1

Library of Congress Cataloging-in-Publication Data
Unwin, Mike.
 The life cycle of reptiles / Mike Unwin.
     p. cm. -- (From egg to adult)
Summary: Discusses how reptiles differ from other animals, what they eat, where they live, how they reproduce, how they survive, and their typical life expectancy.
Includes bibliographical references and index.
 ISBN 1-4034-0781-9 (HC) 1-4034-3408-5 (PB)
 1. Reptiles--Life cycles--Juvenile literature. [1. Reptiles.] I.
Title. II. Series.
 QL644.2 .U69 2003
 597.95--dc21

                    2002011712

Acknowledgments
The Publisher would like to thank the following for permission to reproduce photographs:
p. 4 Bruce Coleman/Gerald S. Cubitt; p. 5 NHPA/Karl Switak; pp. 7 (top), 9, 20, 26 Oxford Scientific Films; p. 7 (bottom) FLPA/E. & D. Hosking; p. 8 Oxford Scientific Films/Mark Deeble; p. 10 NHPA/Nigel J. Dennis; pp. 11, 13 NHPA/Anthony Bannister; p. 12 Oxford Scientific Films/Breck P. Kent; p. 14 Oxford Scientific Films/Tom Ulrich; pp. 15, 17 (top) NHPA/Stephen Dalton; pp. 16 (top), 16 (bottom), 24 NHPA; p. 17 (bottom) FPLA/K. Aitken/Panda; p. 18 Corbis; p. 19 Ardea/Frank Woerle; p. 21 Ardea/Adrian Warren; p. 22 Bruce Coleman Collection/Fred Bruemmer; p. 23 FLPA; p. 25 Australia Zoo; p. 26 (top) NHPA/Daniel Heuclin; p. 29 FLPA/Albert Visage.

Cover photograph of the hatching turtle, reproduced with permission of Oxford Scientific Films.

The lizard at the top of each page is a water dragon.

Every effort has been made to contact copyright holders of any material reproduced in this book. Any omissions will be rectified in subsequent printings if notice is given to the Publishers.

Some words are shown in bold, **like this.** You can find out what they mean by looking in the glossary.

Contents

Look but don't touch: Many reptiles are very easily hurt, and some can also be dangerous. If you see one in the wild, do not get too close to it. Look at it, but do not try to touch it!

What Is a Reptile?

Reptiles are **vertebrates.** Their bodies are supported by skeletons of bones inside their bodies, called **endoskeletons,** and they breathe air through lungs. Their skin is dry, waterproof, and covered in **scales**—very different from the cold, wet skin of amphibians. There are more than 6,500 **species** of reptiles, including snakes, lizards, turtles, tortoises, and crocodiles.

Living dinosaur

Dinosaurs were reptiles that lived on Earth long before people. Today, the tuatara is a living relative of the dinosaurs. This lizardlike reptile has hardly changed since it first appeared 200 million years ago, even though all its relatives have long since become **extinct.**

Warming up

Reptiles are sometimes described as cold-blooded, but their blood is not always cold. In fact, their body temperature changes according to the temperature outside. Reptiles use sunshine to warm up their bodies and give themselves energy. This is why reptiles are more common in warmer parts of the world.

The tuatara lives in rabbit **burrows** *on small islands off the coast of New Zealand.*

How Are Reptiles Born?

Most reptiles lay eggs. Tortoise and crocodile eggs have hard shells, just like bird eggs. Snake, lizard, and sea turtle eggs have soft, leathery shells. Some reptiles, such as geckos, lay only one or two eggs. Others, such as turtles and crocodiles, may lay more than 100. Reptile eggs are on the menu for many animals, including storks, raccoons, and mongooses. Reptiles with the most **predators** lay the most eggs. This gives more of their babies a chance to survive.

Life in the shell

The baby reptile inside the egg, called an **embryo,** gets its food from the **yolk.** A liquid called **amniotic fluid** protects the embryo and yolk. Tiny holes in the eggshell, called pores, let in enough **oxygen** for the baby to breathe.

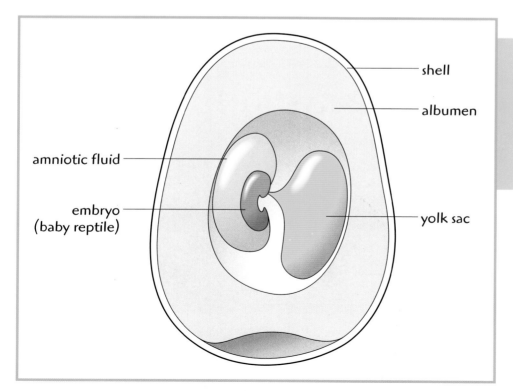

shell

albumen

amniotic fluid

embryo
(baby reptile)

yolk sac

This drawing shows the parts of a growing reptile egg.

5

Keeping eggs warm

Reptile eggs must be kept at just the right temperature for the babies inside to grow. This is called **incubation.** Most reptiles choose a warm, moist place to lay their eggs, such as under a log or buried in the sand or soil. The temperature inside an egg determines whether the baby grows into a male or female. In crocodiles, a temperature of 87 °F to 93 °F (31 °C to 34 °C) produces male babies. A temperature of 79 °F to 86 °F (26 °C to 30 °C) produces females. For turtles and tortoises it is the other way around.

Most female reptiles leave their eggs to incubate and hatch on their own. Others, though, such as pythons and crocodiles, stay with their eggs. They keep the eggs warm and protect them until they hatch.

A female green tree python coils tightly around her eggs to help keep them warm.

Breaking free

To help it get out, each baby reptile has a special sharp egg tooth, which it uses to slice a hole in the shell. It then wriggles and pushes its way outside. The egg tooth of baby crocodiles and tortoises is on the end of their nose. The egg tooth of snakes and lizards sticks out from their upper lip. Egg teeth drop off a few weeks after the babies hatch.

This baby turtle has broken through its shell with its egg tooth.

Live young

Some snakes and lizards that live in cooler parts of the world give birth to live babies instead of laying eggs. This means the **embryo** can develop inside the body of the mother, where it gets all the **nourishment** it needs to grow.

The adder lives in cooler climates than most snakes. It gives birth to about twenty live young. They stay with their mother for a few days before heading off on their own to find food.

Ready to go

Unlike many baby **mammals** and birds, baby reptiles can see, move around, and eat as soon as they are born. They look just like small adult reptiles, but with brighter, shinier colors. Some babies are born with special markings, which disappear when they get older. These colors help to protect them.

A baby crocodile weighs only 9 ounces (250 grams) when it hatches, but its mother may weigh 1,100 pounds (500 kilograms)— more than 2,000 times heavier. This young crocodile is lying on its mother's foot!

Most small reptiles have large babies. A newly hatched baby gecko is about 2 inches (5 centimeters) long. That is about one-third the length of its full-grown mother. Big reptiles have smaller babies.

Who Takes Care of Baby Reptiles?

Most baby reptiles never see their mothers—unlike baby mammals, whose mothers stay with them while they grow up. Some baby snakes stay near their mother for a few days, but she soon leaves, and they have to start taking care of themselves.

Scramble for the sea

A female sea turtle comes ashore to bury her eggs in the dry sand at the top of a beach. There they are hidden from **predators,** and the waves will not wash them away. When the eggs hatch 56 days later, she is nowhere near. The babies dig their way out of the sand at night and hurry down the beach to the sea. On the beach, predators such as crabs, dogs, and vultures wait for them. Sharks lurk in the shallow water. Many baby turtles are eaten. Very few live to adulthood.

Baby hawksbill turtles are only 2 inches (5 centimeters) long. As soon as they hatch, they have to cross the beach and get out to sea as quickly as they can to avoid danger.

Battle for survival

On average, a green turtle lays 1,800 eggs in its lifetime. Unfortunately, most of them never reach adulthood. About 1,400 eggs never hatch, 200 **hatchlings** die on the beach, 160 hatchlings die in the shallows, and 37 hatchlings die in their first week at sea. Only 3 of the baby turtles will survive to become adult turtles.

Caring crocs

Crocodiles are among the few reptiles that care for their babies. A female Nile crocodile guards her nest until the eggs hatch. She does not eat at all during this time. After 90 days, the young crocodiles start squeaking inside their eggs. When the female hears this noise, she opens up the nest, picks up the babies in her mouth, and gently carries them down to the water. She stays close by to protect them for the first six to eight weeks of their lives.

People once thought that female crocodiles ate their babies because of the way they carry them in their mouths. They are, however, very gentle with them, and the babies are not harmed.

How Do Baby Reptiles Grow Bigger?

Reptiles start life small. Inside the egg, the **yolk** gave them all the **nourishment** they needed. This helps them to survive for a short while after hatching, but soon they need to eat in order to grow. Unlike **mammals,** reptiles cannot produce milk for their babies, so the babies have to start finding food for themselves right away.

What's on the menu?

All snakes are **carnivores,** or meat eaters that hunt other animals for food. Some, such as the king cobra, even eat other snakes. Many lizards are **omnivores,** eating a diet of fruit and insects. Only tortoises are true **herbivores.** Their heavy shells make them too slow to catch other animals, so they feed entirely on plants.

*Tortoises are plant eaters. They sometimes also gnaw on rocks that contain a **mineral** called calcium. Calcium helps their shells grow and makes their eggshells stronger.*

Little Killers

Baby reptiles do not have to learn how to find food. Instead, they are born with all the skills they need. A baby rattlesnake knows how to kill its **prey** as soon as it is born. It has enough poison to kill a rat, though at this age it is too small to swallow rats. Instead, it hunts smaller prey, such as grasshoppers.

Just like an adult, a baby southern copperhead uses poison to kill its prey before swallowing it.

A bigger bite

A baby alligator is about 10 inches (25 centimeters) long when it hatches. At this size it eats mostly insects and worms. When it reaches about 3 feet (1 meter) long, it can catch frogs and small fish. At 6 $\frac{1}{2}$ feet (2 meters) long, it can eat larger fish, water birds, and rodents, such as rats. At more than 10 feet (3 meters), a full-grown alligator is big enough to catch a wild pig.

A change of food

As reptiles grow older, their choice of food changes. A baby green turtle starts life as a **carnivore,** eating fish and other small sea creatures. It grows up to become an **herbivore,** eating mostly sea grass.

New skin for old

As a snake or lizard grows bigger, its old, dry skin peels off to reveal shiny new skin underneath. This is called **molting.** Molting first happens a few days after the reptile is born. Most snakes molt three or four times a year, and each time it takes two to three days. A snake's skin comes off in one long piece, but a lizard's peels away in ragged flakes and patches.

During molting, a snake's eyes turn milky white. This happens because a layer of fluid is trapped between the covering of the old eye and the new one. The snake cannot see until the old skin comes off. The snake shown here is a sand snake.

13

Molting safely

A snake finds a safe, hidden spot to **molt.** It starts by rubbing its head against a rock or hard object to loosen the scales around its mouth. It then crawls slowly forward so the rest of the old skin gradually rolls back and comes off inside out. Sea snakes rub against their own coils, so the old skin comes off in a twisted knot.

Baby's rattle

A rattlesnake's rattle is made of many loose pieces of old skin that make a rattling noise when the snake vibrates its tail. A baby rattlesnake is born without a rattle. It has just one small button on the end of its tail. Each time it molts, another piece is added to the button. In this way, the rattle becomes bigger as the snake grows.

A rattlesnake's rattle is made of old, dead skin.
*The noise it makes scares off **predators.***

How Do Reptiles Grow Up Safely?

Most reptiles don't travel very far. Once a young reptile has found a safe, sheltered home, it may stay there for the rest of its life. Most reptiles make their home in a hidden place. Some snakes live in a hole in the ground. Many lizards prefer a crack in a rock or wall. Tortoises live in a clump of grass or a low bush.

Dealing with danger

Life, even with a safe home, is still dangerous for young reptiles. Young reptiles that manage to escape from danger learn to be more careful in the future. As they grow older, they become better at running, hiding, and fighting. This helps them stay alive.

A wall makes a perfect home for baby wall lizards. They can hide in the cracks or bask on the warm stones. There is plenty of insect food nearby, too.

Fooling the enemy

If they are attacked, some young reptiles put on a show to fool their enemies and give them time to get away. A grass snake rolls over on its back and pretends to be dead, so that a **predator** loses interest. Some lizards even lose their tails when they are caught. The tail keeps wriggling to keep the attacker busy while the lizard runs away to safety. Most lizards can grow a new tail. This is known as **regeneration.**

When trapped by a predator, a frilled lizard spreads a frill of skin like an umbrella around its neck to look bigger. It also opens its mouth wide to look more fierce.

When danger threatens, the armadillo girdled lizard ducks into a crack in a rock. If it is caught with nowhere to hide, it rolls itself into a spiky ball by gripping its tail between its teeth. It looks very difficult to swallow, so often a predator leaves it alone.

You can't see me

Some reptiles are so well **camouflaged** that they can hide right out in the open. The leaf–tailed gecko is colored exactly like the bark of a tree. It rests against the trunk with its head pointing downward, waiting to snap up its insect **prey.** Its flat tail and toes and the fringe of skin around its body are flattened against the bark, making it almost impossible to see. If a predator gets too close, the gecko scares it away by suddenly opening its mouth wide to show the bright orange lining.

Can you spot the lizard? The leaf–tailed gecko of Madagascar is so well camouflaged that it is difficult to see.

Life at sea

The olive sea snake spends its life at sea, where it hunts small fish near the surface. It has no permanent home and never comes to land. It sleeps, rests, and gives birth to its babies underwater.

When Is a Reptile Grown Up?

A reptile is grown up when it is ready to start **breeding,** or having babies. Different reptiles grow up at different rates. Dwarf chameleons are ready to breed in nine months. Crocodiles may not be ready for twelve to fifteen years.

Climate differences

The rate at which a reptile grows up depends upon the **climate** where it lives. Reptiles that live in cool climates grow fast during summer but stop growing during winter. In winter, it is too cold for many reptiles to be outside, so they find a warm place to **hibernate.** This means that they take a long rest and don't eat anything or grow at all until spring.

*Red-eared turtles hibernate in the mud at the bottom of ponds. Their body processes slow down, so they do not need to breathe much. They get the little **oxygen** they need from the water through an opening under their bodies.*

Speeding up

Most snakes grow very fast at first. Rattlesnakes that are born in summer have to eat as much food as they can before their long winter hibernation. A timber rattlesnake can double its length in the first year of its life, and it is fully grown after four years. Snakes that live in warm climates don't have to hibernate, so they grow all year round. A young python can grow three times its length during its first year of life.

Slowing down

As reptiles get older, they grow more slowly. They don't need as much energy, so they eat less often. A full-grown African rock python may eat fewer than ten times per year. One big meal, such as an antelope, may take months to **digest.**

A full-grown water python can swallow a whole duck. By changing the position of its flexible jawbones, it can open its mouth wide enough to swallow such a huge meal headfirst.

How Do Reptiles Have Babies?

Once reptiles are grown up, males and females get together to **breed.** First they must find each other. Some reptiles do this by smell. During the breeding season, the special time for mating, a female snake leaves a trail for the male to follow. He uses his tongue to pick up tiny particles of her scent from the air. A special **organ** in the roof of his mouth—called the Jacobson's organ—tells him they belong to a female. Other reptiles use colors. Some male lizards display their bright patterns to females to show they are ready for breeding.

The male anole lizard, from Central America, perches on a tree trunk, puffs out his bright orange throat, and nods his head up and down. This attracts the attention of a female. It also warns rival males to stay away.

Making a noise

Most reptiles are silent, but a few use noises in the breeding season to attract a mate. Male crocodiles thrash the water with their tails, spout jets of water out of their nostrils, and raise their heads to bellow like bulls. Male barking geckos call from the entrances of their desert **burrows.** Their sharp clicking sound carries a long way in the still night air.

Black mambas are poisonous snakes, but the males never bite each other when they fight. Instead, they have long wrestling matches.

Wrestling matches

Some male reptiles compete for females in a battle of strength. Females choose to mate with the winners, whose strength is then passed on to their babies. Male monitor lizards rear up on their hind legs and wrestle. Male tortoises push and bump each other until sometimes one flips the other onto his back. Several male anacondas struggle with each other in one big wriggling ball, but only one of them will mate with the female and **fertilize** her eggs.

Mating dances

Before a male snake can mate with a female, he must get her interested. He moves his body over hers, rubbing his chin along her back and sides and flicking his tongue in and out. In some kinds of snakes, such as cobras, a male and female will rear up and sway together in a **courtship** dance. This goes on until the female gives a sign that she is ready. Then the male wraps himself around her so mating can take place.

*Thousands of Canadian garter snakes **hibernate** together in underground dens to escape the cold. When they wake up in spring, they are ready for mating. For a few days, the ground is covered in wriggling snakes, as all the males struggle to mate with the females at the same time.*

Nesting

When reptiles have mated, the female must find a suitable place to lay her eggs. This is usually a warm, hidden spot, such as inside a hollow tree or under a rock. Some snakes return to use their favorite spot every year. A female king cobra makes a nest of her own. She scoops up a mound of rotting plants and digs two chambers inside. She lays her eggs in the bottom one, then she coils herself up in the top. This keeps the eggs warm underneath her.

Helpful termites

Termites are insects that live in big mounds made of mud. A female water monitor lays her eggs inside a termite mound. The termites then repair the hole she has made. Inside, the eggs are protected, and they stay at just the right warm temperature for **incubation.** At the start of the rainy season, the eggs hatch, and the baby monitor lizards dig their way out.

It takes a female water monitor 2 to 3 days to lay up to 60 eggs inside a termite mound.

Coming home

Sea turtles return to breed on the beaches where they were born. They travel long distances across the ocean, using currents to guide them. **Courtship** and mating take place in shallow water. Then, one moonless night when **predators** on the beach cannot see them, the females come ashore to lay their eggs. They dig a pit above the **high tide line,** beyond the waves, lay their eggs, and cover them with sand. Then they crawl back to the sea and swim away.

Hidden eggs

Like turtles, female tortoises bury their eggs. They dig a long pit in the ground, lay their eggs inside, cover them with soil, and then use their bodies to pack the soil down. Soon there is no sign of the hidden eggs.

It takes two hours for a loggerhead turtle to lay her eggs, cover them, and return to the sea. She will not come back for at least another three years.

How Long Do Reptiles Live?

Many reptiles die young, when life is most dangerous for them. If they escape predators, though, some can live for a very long time. Big reptiles live their lives very slowly. They don't use up much energy, so they are able to live longer. Some geckos can live for more than 25 years—much longer than a mouse or bird of the same size. This chart shows how long different reptiles can live.

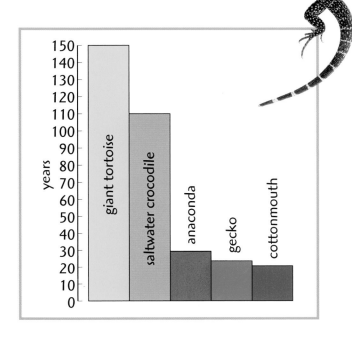

Old-age giants

Reptiles never stop growing, and some get very large. Old leatherback turtles can weigh more than 1,800 pounds (800 kilograms). The oldest saltwater crocodiles can grow more than 20 feet (6 meters) long and weigh more than 1.2 short tons (1 metric ton). Giant tortoises are the longest-living animals. Because they eat only plants, they use very little energy to find food. Their great size and thick shells protect them from predators.

The famous English scientist Charles Darwin saw giant tortoises when he visited the Galápagos Islands in 1833. One tortoise that he brought back is still alive today, and living in Australia. Her name is Harriet, and she is more than 170 years old!

People and reptiles

Most reptiles are perfectly harmless to people. Some reptiles even help people in one way or another. For example, snakes help keep down the numbers of rats and mice that damage farmers' crops. But, despite the harmless nature of reptiles, the future of many **species** is threatened.

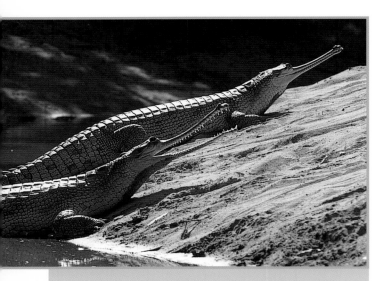

*The gavial, a rare relative of the crocodile, lives in Nepal. It has been hunted close to **extinction.***

Some species, such as crocodiles, pythons, and turtles, are hunted for their skins. Many other species are threatened because people are destroying their **habitats** by cutting down forests and polluting the oceans.

*In the Mediterranean, noisy discos and bright hotel lights have scared away turtles from many of the beaches where they used to **breed.***

The cycle of life

No reptile lives forever. Even so, by the time an adult reptile dies, it will have helped bring many more of its kind into the world. Over a lifetime, a female reptile, such as a turtle, may lay hundreds of eggs. Not all the eggs hatch, and many **hatchlings** die young. But those that live through all the dangers of life, such as **predators** and pollution, may one day grow up to breed themselves. This is the cycle of life—from egg to adult—in which young are born, grow, and produce young themselves. The cycle of life ensures the survival of each reptile species.

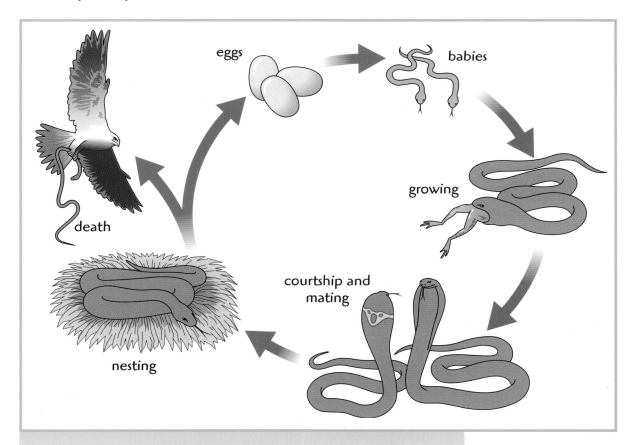

All reptiles pass through the same stages in their life—from egg to adult.

Fact File

What is . . .

• the biggest family?

Sea turtles lay the most eggs of any reptile. A leatherback turtle lays up to 1,000 eggs in batches of 100 to 120 during 11-day intervals. She then waits 2 to 5 years before **breeding** again.

• the biggest egg?

Pythons lay the biggest eggs of any reptile. They are round in shape, and about 4 inches (10 centimeters) around—roughly the size of an orange.

• the most babies ever given birth to?

Some snakes can have a lot of live young. The record for any reptile is held by a puff adder from Kenya, which gave birth to 156 babies.

• the longest incubation?

The eggs of some lizards may **incubate** for over a year if development slows down during winter. Some chameleon eggs can take 377 days to hatch. In captivity, where the incubation temperature is kept exactly right all the time, they take about half this time.

• the biggest reptile?

It is hard to be sure how big reptiles can grow in the wild. The longest known snake is the reticulated python of Southeast Asia, which occasionally reaches 30 feet (9 meters). Big leatherback turtles can weigh more than 2,000 pounds (900 kilograms). The largest reptile is the saltwater crocodile, which may weigh more than 1.2 short tons (1 metric ton) and measure 23 feet (7 meters) long.

Reptile Classification

Classification is the way scientists group living things. They divide all the reptiles in the world into four main groups.

- The biggest group of reptiles is the scaled reptiles, which includes snakes and lizards. There are more than 6,200 different **species.** They all have teeth and **molt** their dry, scaly skin. Snakes and some kinds of lizards have no legs.
- The second group is the shield reptiles, which includes tortoises, turtles, and terrapins. There are 273 different species. They all have a hard protective shell, four legs, and a horny beak instead of teeth.
- The third group of reptiles is the crocodiles and alligators. There are 23 different species. They all have tough skin covered in horny plates, long tails, and four legs. Their long jaws have sharp teeth.
- There are only two species of tuataras in the fourth group. These lizardlike reptiles have four legs, a long tail, and soft, scaly skin. Their skeleton shows that they have changed little in 200 million years.

The Komodo dragon, of Indonesia, is the world's biggest lizard. It measures up to 10 feet (3 meters) long, and weighs up to 350 pounds (160 kilograms)— big enough to catch and eat a goat.

Glossary

amniotic fluid thick liquid inside an egg that protects the embryo

breed have babies

burrows underground animal homes

camouflage color or pattern that helps an animal blend in with its background

carnivore meat-eating animal

climate usual kind of weather in one place. For example, the Amazon rain forest has a warm, wet climate.

courtship special behavior that takes place before mating

digest to break down food in the body so that it can be used for energy

embryo very first stage of an animal's life, when it is still developing inside the egg

endoskeleton skeleton of bones inside an animal's body

extinct/extinction word describing an animal or plant that has died out and disappeared from Earth forever

fertilization/fertilize When an egg is fertilized, an embryo begins to grow inside.

habitat natural home of any living thing. A Nile crocodile's habitat is freshwater rivers.

hatchling baby animal when it has just hatched out of its egg

herbivore animal that eats just plants

hibernation/hibernate long period of winter rest, when it is very cold or there is not enough food

high tide line highest point that waves reach on a beach

incubation/incubate keeping an egg at the correct temperature for the baby inside to grow

mammals warm-blooded animals with a backbone that feed their young on milk from the mother's body

migration/migrate seasonal journey of animals from one place to another in order to find food or a good place for breeding

mineral chemical in the ground or in food, such as iron or calcium, that is important for growth

molting the peeling off of an outer layer of skin from the body when it has become worn out

nourishment goodness and energy that comes from eating food

omnivore animal that eats plants and meat

organ part of the body that has a special job

oxygen gas in the air and dissolved in water that living things need to breathe

predator animal that hunts and eats other animals for food

prey animal that is hunted and eaten by a predator

regeneration growing something again.

scale small, flat piece on an animal's skin that is tough like fingernails

species group of living things that are similar in many ways and can breed to produce healthy babies

vertebrate animal with a backbone. Mammals, birds, reptiles, amphibians, and fish are all vertebrates.

yolk part of an egg that serves as food for the growing baby inside

More Books to Read

Catala, Ellen. *Venomous Snakes.* Broomall, Penn.: Chelsea House Publishers, 2003.

Facklam, Margery. *Lizards: Weird and Wonderful.* New York: Little Brown Books, 2003.

Gareth Stevens Publishing Staff. *Reptiles.* Milwaukee, Wisc.: Gareth Stevens, Inc., 2002.

Holden, Henry M. *The American Alligator.* Berkely Heights, N.J.: Enslow Publishers, Inc., 2003.

Miller, Chuck. *Tortoises.* Austin, Tex.: Raintree Publishers, 2002.

Miller, Sara Swan. *Radical Reptiles.* Danbury, Conn.: Scholastic Library Publishing, 2001.

Trueit, Trudy Strain. *Snakes.* Danbury, Conn.: Scholastic Library Publishing, 2003.

Welsbacher, Anne. *Komodo Dragons.* Minnetonka, Minn.: Capstone Press, Inc., 2002.

Index